A Gallery of Ghosts

Cover: J.M.W Turner, *Europa and the Bull*, ca. 1840-50, oil on canvas, 35-7/8 x 47-7/8 in. (91.1 x 121.6 cm), Bequest of Charles Phelps and Anna Sinton Taft, Taft Museum of Art, Cincinnati, Ohio. Reproduced by permission.

Back Cover Photo by Biljana Obradovic

Book design by Bill Lavender

ISBN: 0-9728143-4-5
ISBN 13: 978-0-9728143-4-8

Managing Editor
Bill Lavender

University of New Orleans Publishing
UNO Metro College
New Orleans, LA   70148
http://unopress.uno.edu

Acknowledgments

Some of these poems (sometimes in different versions) have appeared in the following journals. The author wishes to acknowledge and thank their editors for permission to reprint the poems:

Cumberland Poetry Review: "The Day after Labor Day" and "Directions for Surprise"; *Descant*: "Conceit for My Cancer" and "Last Loss"; *Die Young*: "Genealogue"; *Edge City Review*: "Leaf Like Love"; *Ekphrasis*: "Paraclete Almost"; *Ellipsis*: "Lines for an Obstinate Poet" and "The Panthers of Worry"; *George Washington Review*: "After the Facts"; *Icarus International: Roll, Pitch, & Yaw*: "The Wandering of Amelia Earhart as a Model for Our Time"; *Interdisciplinary Humanities*: "At God's Apartment"; *The Iowa Review*: "Two Mississippis"; *Kenyon Review*: "Lie #4: That Frances Osgood Slept with E.A. Poe" and "Lie #6: That Hart Crane Crawled in Bed between the Cowleys"; *Louisiana Literature*: "Giving Up the Ghost," "Night Glimpse," and "Stump"; *Neovictorian*: "The Empty Staircase," "Your Average Piecework," and "The Wrong Tormented Sea"; *New Orleans Review*: "Unemployment"; *Paris Review*: "Lie #1: That Penelope Resisted Scores of Suitors" and "Lie #2: That Parkman Almost Died on the Oregon Trail"; *Pivot*: "Promises"; *Sparrow*: "Bachelor of Arts" and "An Undisclosed Source"; *The Southern Anthology*: "Lie #9: That Oswald Was a Cuban Sympathizer" and "Munich Evening: After the Reunification of Germany"; *Spirit*: "Promiscuous Spirit," "Making Decisions," and "For the Duration"; *Verse*: "Poem for Barbara" and "Between"; *Wallace Stevens Journal*: "Speech for the Wallace Stevens Society"; *War, Literature, and The Arts*: "Lie #5: That Babe Ruth Pointed Out That Famous Homer," "Lie #8: That 'Little Boy' Saved Half a Million Lives," and "Lie #10: The Patriot Missiles Freed the Persian Gulf"; *West Branch*: "Lie #7: That Scott Fitzgerald Sent Himself a Postcard."

"Ineptitude" (as "Ineptness") first appeared in *Maple Leaf Rag II: 15th Anniversary Anthology* (Portals Press, 1995); "No Elegy for One Who Died Too Soon" originally appeared in *Something In Common: Louisiana Poets*, ed. Ann Dobie (Louisiana State University Press, 1998); "Poem for Barbara" was reprinted in *Gulf Coast Collection Of Poems And Stories*, eds. James P. White and Jeff Todd (Texas Center for Writers Press, 1994). "Two Mississippis" was filmed and produced by Aaron Rushin as a video in the series *Poets in the Dream State* (New Orleans Video Access, 2002). Seventeen of these poems also appear in my book, *American Ghost: Selected Poems*, translated into Serbian by Biljana D. Obradovic (Raska Skola, 1999; Cross-Cultural Communications, 1999).

The author also acknowledges the National Endowment for the Arts for a Creative Writing Fellowship, the Cummington Community for the Arts for an Artist's Residency, and the University of New Orleans College of Liberal Arts for a Summer Scholar Award as well as sabbatical leave, all of which provided time and resources toward the completion of this collection. Also, sincere thanks to Maxine Cassin for her valuable editorial comments and to Joseph Bednarik and Dana Gioia for their sustaining advice and encouragement.

A Gallery of Ghosts

John Gery

Contents

Landscapes

Still Lives

About the Poet

What heart heard of, ghost guessed

—G.M. Hopkins

Promiscuous Spirit

I've been searching through this crowd of wild women
for you, your hair dripping to your shoulders
like water through trees after rain, but where
in this cross-town traffic, among the clutter
of buses, the bees serenading the twilit streets,
have you concealed your generous palpability?
Why do you keep yourself so indiscreetly
without, while behind these drawn blinds
where I sometimes live, within the white heart
of the world of my little belonging, I turn
around and around the words I would win you by
to stay? Is it the husk of my shorn dream
that frightens you? Is it the long rein
of the divine, the battering bartering rip
of adorned bodies I don't know, have never known,
the sad call of small bass in the last lakes
no one has stopped from draining that draws you
away and away? Have the trees lost their shadows,
the air its nonchalance, the earth its look of fear?

Too old, too old to hold two breasts believing,
This is the best so leave the rest alone,
I round out various sounds you say and lay them
at your feet like beads, in hope you won't notice
other than the gentle muscle of my need.
I want to plant a seed not in the sand
our bodies and the trees will be buried with
but in that red stream we come to, familiarly,
to praise, with music mostly in mind
or that quietness no music can replace.
Where is your face? Where is your sign?

Sketches & Abstractions

Stranger: It is difficult, my dear Socrates, to demonstrate anything of real importance without the use of examples.

—Plato, *Statesman*

Promises

Arriving like unsolicited mail
or propositions from women
who mean well, they surprise me

as though I get to go to Mexico
and no one will be the wiser for it.
Together with my own lies

and the magic of sudden tears
bursting with riches
like broken piñatas, they comprise

years of my wasted inside life.
Even now, as I start to talk
about them, I taste their lactose

and curse my fat tongue
for shaping words whose sweets
will betray me. Take one

into your mouth. Suck hard
on its orbicular curves. Feel
how your nerves rise, then blur,

comforted by a candied future
you can take full measure of
only when it diminishes, melting

like a slow kiss. I love this,
this proliferation of sins
to savor, the blending to none.

Making Decisions

If you pick just one out of this flock
and try to keep your focus on it,
the way a ray of light follows the glint
on a woman's necklace, no matter
that she wanders uptown or through the park,

and if, when the flock dissolves, or a few,
chattering, settle in trees, you identify yours
by its ragged crest, its fluid dip and fall
the moment it spots a scrap on the ground
to snap up, or how it trails the slow crawl
of land prey,

                    you still can't be sure
it is the same one you first saw and said,
Mine, for now. In fact, were it not
for your knack of failing in resolve
when put to the test by laws or friends,
not so clever as the cat who licks its paws

before pouncing, you could admit
to this flaw yet go on
watching the sky for assistance, calling it
a necessary business, however false.

Speech for the Wallace Stevens Society

We agree, then, that the particular
like a lump of chemical disinfectant
is deadly—or, at least, death-inducing—

as though in our mild attempt to clean house
it poisoned the lot of us and we went cheerfully
under, part way toward some broader appeal.

At a bargain price, too! These things we buy,
you know, may last forever, if we don't
actually use them. But if we do they kill us

with their smell of immortality.
                              Now, it's not
that I want to be a valetudinarian,
since I haven't swallowed the modern pill, not yet

anyway. And what of the pleasures of reclining
casually in the company of friends you can count
on one hand, their smiles warm and wavy?

Afterwards, you're liable to feel a tinge
of general well-being, the way a salt bath
tempers the nerves, little by little,

seeping slowly into your skin like high fashion,
or a sunburn after a day at the beach. In fact,
an idea, for all its unique properties

only strong lotions can entirely block,
might stay with you into the next season,
not just as a line you admire when the two of you,

lying naked next to each other, try to measure how far
you've come together, but as an urge as new as cells
in your limbs, gayly playing with themselves until,

with the inevitability of a used car, they die.
Yet as I've said, here is something we can agree on,
like the lift of a window in winter, our theme.

Unemployment

This uselessness arrests you
like the highway police.
Who's speeding?
you wonder at first
but before you've put away
that part of you assignable,
stacked neatly in your
efficient brain, something
as mysterious as sleep
drags you from this wheel
you've clutched so long
and holds you in contempt.

You plead, your whole face
twisted in disbelief
at such an unbecoming turn
of events. Then you pluck
whatever has gotten you
this far—compliments,
good works, physical love.

But uselessness takes you on
to chaos, justice
of the peace, who will not
let you go. Nor
will your bootless cries
trouble a deft heaven,
clever enough to have put
plenty of unknowns between
you and it, thick layers
of consciousness as hazy

as chalk, its laws full
of directions you can't
possibly need, as you wait,
delayed, for whatever creep
has made this happen.

The Panthers of Worry

for John Cooke

The panthers outside my window,
sleek, pace for a meal.
When I hear them, I feel weak
anticipating the chase. Why

in the give-and-take of sleep
won't they heel, in this case,
granting my appeal to fate
to keep me from coming awake

having to wear this face again?
Driven by unknown crimes, I
break from bed yet soon recline
without fever or answers.

My panthers have acquired a taste
for a carcass they smell alive.
One brief leap and they're
inside, tearing at my meat,

and I won't be surprised if,
after their quick retreat,
the vultures of dread arrive
to pluck from my eyes

what few sad pieces my panthers
leave behind: like sighs of regret
I've never quite sighed
or things undone, things unsaid.

Ineptitude

How could I lead my life without these words
    to stay my grief? How could I trade
    for one night's sleep what even birds
themselves, in frenzied singing overhead, have made

of all this shit they've seen? Sometimes supposing
    my private ignorance and pain
    the consequence of inept dozing,
I stir up small sound waves around me to sustain

even their slightest flutter, as though my pulse
    were worth repeating in a verse
    to keep whatever doom that dulls
the senses from eradicating mine, or worse

from bursting like a dream. Yet in the end
    I've not created anything
    but noise, an empty dividend
though one that has a terribly familiar ring.

A Sign along the Way

(On the Problem of "Did You See That?")

If this is meaningless only to those who read
what it says, by what means do they say

how they know? Or do we know what they mean,
in passing, billboard bending from view,

between the saying it has for those who read it
and whatever, as we imagine they will tell us,

is to be remembered? Of the others here,
who mean nothing by their silence—only

what fares between before, when they thought
they knew what was meant, and later

as they struggle to remember—we can say
practically as much. But who will read, beyond

those trees, after they argue it is meaningless,
what by then will have passed us by?

No one. And this is important, not
because what it says when they read it

is to be remembered, further down the freeway,
nor because what fares between us, who thought

saying was meaning, meant practically
as much as the others' silence, but because,

later, without it we will not have said
all we know, as whatever we thought we read,

and since believing must also mean imagining,
we can only go forward with this in mind.

An Image for Someone's Opinion I Don't Quite Follow

She is an angelfish nibbling the coral
who eats little and rarely hungers
other than when riddled by sunlight
plunging through the surf. A fresh current
replenishes her reef and suddenly, like grief,
washes her backwards into the other fish.

Were she to wish, she might wish this:
That the darters wouldn't splash her
away from the red edges she lunges toward.
That her school would stay still somehow
in the cross stream, and glean from the sea
what's best to eat. That her colors
would glow more, not in blue or yellow,
but as glaireous as an egg-sack
scattering across an open sound.

Clarity

Always, it sneaks up like a headache. First
I notice at the edges of my brain
    a pressure small as Switzerland.
My sockets start swelling up. Then a thirst
(or salivating tongue) begins to drain
    my throat until a flushed command

of blood rushes the borders of my skull,
while a throbbing, north to south, like contraband
    smuggled across a mountaintop,
crawls through my eyes, slowing down to a lull
until, suddenly, as I lift my hand
    to lock my temples in, and crop

the tree line on my forehead's Dolomites,
a consciousness of consciousness breaks through!
    Vast spaces open, packed with pain
palpable as snow, encircled by lights
and bells. Like this, one thought bolts into view—
    until, like that, it's gone again.

Directions for Surprise

If it arrives like a box in your absence, be pleased
with yourself, for your having had no idea,
its very indignity a trigger to gratitude
like a vote by Congress to feed the hungry
while you've been doing nothing special
all day, just drowsing, staying your own death.
What's this? you wonder. What short breath has been
taken away? What blood drained? What quiet
rises in you in the company of such delight
like the aroma of homemade soup? Or like angels.
Can you turn the next corner, turn any corner

again, never being the same? Whole visions
of satisfied strangers unbuttoning their belts
as they slurp, on long wooden benches, of banners
draped from the arches of your heavenly home,
will gather at your mind's gate, crowding you in.
This leaves little to be desired, and even less
to escape from, like a clean glass of water
or the smile of one who was once in love with you
renewed now in another room somewhere. Try,
if you can, to express this emptiness
suddenly filled in, and follow your urge to open.

A Pack of Lies

For Jonathan Edwards & Eugene McCarthy, two U.S. servicemen killed
in the Persian Gulf War against Iraq, 1–3 February 1991

There's an Arab saying that when you tell someone that a man has
died, he asks, "Is he dead and buried or is he just dead?"
                                        —Fouad Ajami, journalist

Lie #1: That Penelope Resisted Scores of Suitors

I'm not convinced that woman wanted him
ever to come back home. She had her business
in tapestries, those three-hour meals with men,
and Telemachus, who it's true was dim
and narrow, some said not unlike Ulysses,
but still his mother's toy. And after ten

or more years, don't all lovers seem the same
in memory? One man surmounts the teeming,
well-meaning invitations, only to pout
when she, like Hera, claims she's not to blame
for his interminable lust and dreaming.
The man wants her to take him; she wants out

of the question of desire altogether,
on his terms. So she starts to count completely
not on Ulysses' missing, but on facts
like ships we watch crossing against the weather
toward the world's edge, which shimmer discretely,
then disappear when some small flick distracts

our curious eyes. You couldn't pin her down,
not that one. Cooler to the touch than the prick
of a needle, she had mastered her delay
with vague unweavings, building her renown
on nothing but a calculated trick
to cover black and white with seamless grey,

to keep the fools like me coming around
drooling like basset hounds. It's often so:
The facts protect the ones who want to lie
alone, while those for whom nothing is sound
muddle, splash and drown. Sometimes, though,
we also sail, blindly, into the sky.

Lie #2: That Parkman Almost Died on the Oregon Trail
(The Ogillallah Village, 1846)

My mind is mush. Three days without a thought
but how to tell them I can't eat their corn
again, nor smoke that pipe that tastes like silt,
nor drink the soot in the water bags we brought
from Boston. Why do I think I was born
for something better than this bile I've spilt

on prairie grass, which dies only to sprout
hardier than before? My education
seems now mostly an exercise in tact
and confidence, as though to conquer doubt
I talked myself into thinking a whole nation
of Sioux, Dahcotah, and Blackfeet could be tracked

like body parts drawn in some medical book.
Mornings I read, when I'm not on the trail,
or talk with trappers come down from the Black Hills;
by noon, whatever meaning I mistook
for fact fades, like the buffalo or whale,
so that by night the dark sends up my back chills

worse than a seasick sailor's. *Write it down,*
I keep reminding myself, *Write it down,*
and pray ideas will shoot forth from the earth
I lie on, shivering in my dressing gown.
But nausea engulfs me and I drown
in ignorance and colic fits not worth

Harvard Library's crowded shelves of lies:
Even the idea I do not belong here,
once noted, seems banal against this beauty
I couldn't have predicted would hurt my eyes,
and dreading what I'm eating seems the wrong fear.
Maybe a lack of sleep has made me moody

or working hard to mispronounce their words,
to prove myself both flexible and stable,
has skewed the reason why I came: for truth.
I'm small. We're all small. Hardly more than birds.
Whatever I write is nothing but a label
to identify my corpse by, like a tooth.

Lie #3: That Mourning His Wife's Death Killed Mendelssohn

It takes more than a broken heart to die
alone. It takes lifting the hand that plunges
the sword, like Hamlet's through Laertes's chest,
and drinking poison with it to sense why
you've ceased to care. It takes distrusting hunches
your own bad luck will turn out for the best

in some just heaven that won't shake you loose.
It takes ignoring the beauty of the wave
you are about to throw yourself against
enraged, before you slip into the sluice
that draws your pain. Most broken hearts behave
not wildly but modestly, like cattle fenced

who wait, indifferent, or the fat rose blooming
among the thousand bred. You need a crowd
to die among, if you are serious.
You can't trudge off to death with dread entombing
your agitated mind, your stomach fouled
by food, your flesh adorned for her you miss.

Maybe, once you recover from your grief,
forgetting friends' advice or fields you've crossed
in pairs, your past a future you no longer need,
you may, bewildered, shiver like a leaf
or acorn, in the unrelenting frost,
and valiantly, the moment you are freed,

drop on the blades under a weeping oak.
The sonatina in your head may please you,
as you float through the autumn air. The sun,
waning in strength, may hold you in its stroke,
engendering a mild breeze to ease you.
And then the damage done may be undone.

Lie #4: That Frances Osgood Slept with E.A. Poe

They say it isn't sex that you remember.
I disagree. To think of Edgar's frown
that night we lay in bed till after five
talking about the future as the ember
beneath the grate flickered, burning down
to nothing—never had I felt alive

like that, I thought, he so preoccupied,
imagining every variant of death
he could, and I determined to give birth
to one of our ideas before I died,
the "curse of poetry" our shibboleth.
But poetry does not disturb the earth:

I can't agree with all that talk of spirit
he made. It's opening my legs, I swear,
ever so slightly while he sucked my breast,
then took my thigh in his left hand to steer it
over his own, coming inside to bear
my hips on his hips, I remember best.

I wouldn't scribble this, were not my eyes
so bleary from the pills and tea, like blood
flushed through a drain, my nurse pours down my throat.
She blinds my body so my soul might rise
invisibly, like smoke above the flood
of longing that slaps against this burning boat,

but I am sinking faster than her hope.
I sense the swirling sea surround me. Hate
I couldn't call it, but despair's the thing
that slowly starts to tighten like a rope,
as fastened to the mainmast of my fate,
I feel its spar inside me still. And still I cling.

Lie #5: That Babe Ruth Pointed Out That Famous Homer

As usual, who knows where this is going?
I met this guy once, damn good public speaker
at sports banquets without no ladies present,
who told me he believed, without quite knowing—
like the gal who runs off only when you seek her—
that fame assures our being obsolescent

by and by. Who thinks of Nefertiti,
for instance, anymore? Her lusts, I mean,
or appetites. Nothing remains in tact,
and even the most monumental treaty
among God-fearing states ain't worth one bean
if everyone just buys it. Still, we act

expecting our gestures to be acted on,
like children who fight their parents, imitating
the action they resist the way *that* action
resembles those by which amoebae spawn.
I always thought of sex when I was dating,
for instance, which became a great distraction

from having to get laid. The gals were pretty
enough—I had this weakness for a dress
and weighed less then than now, my mind awash
in a fog too dense to burn off from the pity
of women—yet the moment to confess
I was as ready as a butter squash

would pass silently, like an evening breeze,
the kind you only notice in the summer
caressing you: You raise an arm, then pray
what you don't know will lift you through the trees
to God. That guy said you can pick a comer
by how he doesn't know the time of day

as well as what he's thinking he might do
with whatever's left of it. I've since forgotten
what else he said—on what you have to lose
by taking risks. The point is that it's true
until your body's in the ground and rotten
your best bet is a temporary ruse.

Lie #6: That Hart Crane Crawled in Bed between the Cowleys

"Exhaustion has become its own reward,"
I said, plopping onto their sheets, as grey
as grebes too filled with ennui to attack.
My life a lark compared to theirs, yet bored
from cruising sailors who drooled like dogs to play
at paradise, I flung across her back

one outstretched arm, then cupped her breast, then drew
the fingers of my right hand down his spine,
who turned to face me, angry though not vexed,
asking, "Now what are we supposed to do?"
"You can't take her alone, I've come for mine,"
I answered, then spread out, not oversexed,

as she claimed later, but in love with them
both. Coupled with responsibilities
to nest all longing in a solo voice,
still, aching that *un homme* might be *une femme*,
I thought of nothing but my urge to please:
Things weren't the way I'd hoped. I had no choice

but to forage the private dreams of friends
for my dreams. Like a mockingbird stealing
the songs it loves, I faked theirs as my own.
Yet theirs could never justify my ends
until, defeated by a lack of feeling,
scrubbing their bone with skin, their skin with bone,

I wore down what they were with what I seemed,
flitting behind my poetry and thin,
belabored schemes. By dropping wings out there
in West Connecticut, as Malcolm squirmed,
I scavenged like a hawk, or peregrine,
and picked apart the flesh of their affair,

a fagging nuisance, while to Peggy I came
insisting like a widgeon on her kindness.
But what if I'm not bird nor fowl but ghoul—
or worse, a mutant thing without a name?
I wish, moaning like Homer in his blindness,
I could invent a hybrid singing school.

Lie #7: That Scott Fitzgerald Sent Himself a Postcard

Missing you, I've traveled the Cote d'Azur
and drunk my way through inns of molten blue,
hoping to glimpse your face in washroom mirrors
or on the brass rail at the Ritz. Obscure
here, where nobody reads *The Smart Set* through
and California's known for neither heroes

nor literati, I can still get lost
the way I always wanted but would fail to
back in St. Paul. So I veered off the highway
and found this ville where two francs gets me sauced
on vin du pays, where no one forwards mail to
and even Jews aren't recognized. In my way

I've buried Scott while sparing Scottie's father.
But why write home to you, then? You're a disgrace.
A wonk who won't desert his work. How sad.
I brought your brains with me but didn't bother
to clue you in. This scene reveals the place
where you can find me now. Don't be a cad:

Look closer! There behind those lemon trees
shimmering in that grove near my chateau
you'll spot your stand-in, hidden like that gun
you stole once from my Stutz, despite my pleas
that you stop interfering. Take the dough
I stashed in Zelda's strongbox. Let's have fun!

Quit torturing yourself. The Goldwyn script
can wait a month or more, can wait a year,
for all they care. Once I believed like you
Americans could profit from being gypped
in love and art. How stupid. Evenings here
a vodka haze of beauty veils the view.

Lie #8: That "Little Boy" Saved Half a Million Lives

Someone proposed we drop it in the sea
to demonstrate how our peace-loving dreams
differed from theirs, but none of us was sure
the thing would splash into that blinding tree
it had above the desert. The harebrained schemes
of Fermi, Lawrence, Oppenheimer, and Bohr

had not inspired fear before, so why,
right after we had passed our greatest test,
crushing the fascists, hesitate or halt,
hoping a few more thousand wouldn't die?
A few more thousand might convince the rest
to realize it was Hirohito's fault,

not ours, that we had had to go this far
to spare them one more Eastern tyranny—
both Genghis Khan and Mao came to mind.
Even that peasant's son, pretender czar,
would have to listen to us. Don't you see?
No treaty could protect us from the blind.

Yet which of us was not blind? Truth be known,
we couldn't guess the casualties to come
with or without the thing. No one was certain.
So like a blind man in a room alone
who moves toward a window, reaching from
not to, both palms turned out, drawing the curtain

to feel the sun's rays streaming through the glass,
we made our way by stumble, clutch, and pry.
We gauged not deaths but decibels of sound
and placed bets on the wind speed of the blast,
then huddled close, none daring prophesy
for good or ill. A few knelt on the ground.

Lie #9: That Oswald Was a Cuban Sympathizer
(24 November 1963)

You think I had a plan, but I was lonely,
wasting those afternoons without a job.
You wouldn't know. So when this fat guy—well,
he wasn't fat, really, just wealthy, only
he wore a baggy, white suit, like that slob
in Moscow—when he spoke about Fidel,

that day we fell to talking on Magazine,
and coaxed me downtown to his union hall,
I had to take the bus. By the time I got there
he'd disappeared. Instead, some fairy queen,
shouting, "They're all God's shit!" began to bawl,
waving his arms and pumping the crowd with hot air

about "The Revolution." What the fuck
did I care? I was out of work, not jargon.
I ate their lunch. Then, two more flaming liars.
And would've left next, but a pick-up truck
parked on Camp Street was hiring at a bargain,
so like those rats that crawl the electric wires

I crept along Canal, handing out leaflets
to all the derelicts and tourists. Well,
not the tourists, since I repulsed them. Always
for me it's been that way. Since you're some chief, it's
damn clear white trash like me can go to hell,
for all you care. But strutting down these hallways

parading me through Dallas to be jailed,
you'll see: They won't excuse Lee Harvey anymore.
Sure, back there in New Orleans, they could pick me
to be their guinea pig, and if I failed
I'd move along and quietly ignore
that no one saw. But here no one can kick me

or make fun of the way I say my name.
I'm just a patsy. But now that I'm theirs
their law protects me just like I was rich.
You wouldn't know that's been my secret game
all along. So fuck you. Go on downstairs.
Then watch my plan come off without a hitch.

Lie #10: That Patriot Missiles Freed the Persian Gulf
(February 1991)

Watching the patriots approach the scuds
like Gyno-cream committing spermicide,
I felt enamored, for a moment, of
America: As bright blasts streamed in floods
of red, inside I almost burst with pride
imagining my body making love

devoid of shame and safe from scattering
debris. But then a scud and patriot fell
together, mingling in a spray of white
and blue, until, spreading in a fatter ring
of green ash, they receded. I could tell,
by looking closer, how the desert night

like tangled sheets lay barren: In one corner
my TV screen next focused on a girl
no older than I am, her garments stripped,
a baby dangling from one arm. She'd born her
away from Baghdad to escape that whirl
of love's machinery, just to be blipped

to General Norman Schwarzkopf's outstretched prong
pointing to holes where oil tanks used to be,
bridges had stood, and soldiers had lain sleeping.
Throughout his briefing, the press laughed at his long
and surgically thorough mastery
of Saddam Hussein's secret places. Leaping

to run away from what she'd seen, she'd seen
enough—the young Iraqi mother, that is—
but so had I, in Cairo, Illinois.
Later, I joined my friends at Dairy Queen
for soft ice cream. I asked them where Kuwait is.
As pleased as I was that my steady boy

had not been blown out of his tent, still I cried,
having decided not to have his child
before he left for war. "It's not the danger,"
I told my friends, "It's that that general lied,
saying no patriot would be defiled.
The one I love is stranger than a stranger."

Self-Portraits

To scan a Ghost, is faint
—Emily Dickinson

From an Undisclosed Source

My own desire is never to be known, yet
to have inhabited the halls of power
like some unnoticed lintel, always there
above the door, whom presidents can't do
without, within all inner conclaves, true
upholder of the holy portiere
of silence, ever narrower and narrower
and wise—until I, once I'm left alone, let

the things I've heard wash over me like rain,
cleansing my anonymity: Who cares,
since no one will remember me, what lies
I spill, what ships of state my leaks capsize,
what dammed secrets burst, drowning my pain?
Oblivion rewards us unawares.

Genealogue

I have no children but plenty of fathers to make up
the difference. It would take another Whitman
to enumerate them, and some say they keep me young,
so many teeth to cut I may never stop talking.

The sweat of them all seeps from every pore
and sometimes I am drowning, drowning, other times
grunting my way back to that first mysterious sperm guy,
that laconic tyrant shuffling through his palace

during the revolution, who mindlessly threw together
for the archivists his favorite sporting clothes
and a few old silver spoons, then rode out the night
into the llano of anonymity where, generations later,

I was born. What secret heirs my flesh is prey to
rock my cradle for attention. They dote on me
with their fresh demands as I gaze and gaze up at them
for the point of all this, for something to hold onto,

some ghostly finger to grab to stop its wag,
while the women who surround them fade and forget,
as they are forgotten, the suck they gave me,
sucked themselves into this barren present.

Three Halves

Not to want children doesn't mean not to want
their parents, even though your having them
is about as likely as where three roads converge
your father will happen by in his new sports car
and, while you lope there, splatter you with mud

before you've even had a chance to recognize him
so you pull out your Luger and blast him away.
In dreams both lust and hatred stay safe
from viscous fear, and everyone calls everyone
by names they're unfamiliar with. But if,

just once, you trust what you've seen and slice,
like a hungry Tereus, into your family meat
without knowing, or fondle your in-laws, sadly
your days will pass, until they arrest you
and book you as a myth: These things happen,

not to me, though, since I'm never altogether
here, half-asleep, half-longing, only half-alone.

Bachelor of Arts

Desiring this man's craft or that man's wife,
without a center of my own to crawl
to, I began at last to see my life
as only part of what it seemed, not all,

so like a bird I watched once at the zoo
lifting the same stick with its beak to fit it
into a nest that wasn't there, I grew
increasingly unnerved—until I bit it

in half, my stick, still imagining a nest
that might need half a twig, or half a bird,
an aviary for the part-possessed.
But nothing's changed, and now my view's so blurred

I'm like a bird that crashes into glass:
I can see through but I can't pass.

The Empty Staircase

Here is the empty staircase in my head.
      Rather than push you through the dark,
I'll light this switch: See how those top slats arc
      like bows pulled taut? Beware that red

glowing behind you, veins frayed to their roots
      from nights of rubbing at my eyes.
They spell out THIS WAY DOWN. Whoever tries
      to mount these steps must fix her boots

to slow her slide and hitch her climber's rope
      to ledges in her own brain. Mine
has collapsed. It's been posted with a sign.
      It reads, CONDEMNED: ABANDON HOPE.

Between

From behind me I can see a version
of myself ahead, my curling shoulder
heaving forward, anxious for occasion
to return my look. It's getting colder.

My Eurydice is disappearing
yet my Orpheus still slumps on, mired
in the mud of dreaming of that clearing
where she'll be the self he has desired.

Which to trust? And why pursue a phantom
time and time again? They both deceive me,
what I am and how I feel, at random,
any moment now likely to leave me,

she back down, he up, the sudden space
I am in their absence, like a breach
of promise, neither faded with her face
nor resurrected by his human speech.

Your Average Piecework

All are needed by each one;
Nothing is fair or good alone.
—*Emerson*

What if my personality
were surgically detached, like so much fat
    cut from thighs too long cushioned
by chocolate, beer and long days sitting at

    some desk? Would anybody notice,
when I entered a room, my sense of humor
    missing? Or if I laughed, would friends,
in treating me as though I'd had a tumor

    removed, not mention it and smile
that grim smile athletes do at those they've beaten
    in the early heats—triumphant, cruel?
The baggy clothes I now hide my conceit in

    I'd throw away, as though to say
this me is me, like you and you and you,
    is nothing richer than a heap
of average piecework—bone, disease, and glue—

    a casual combination of
divine wet meat, which I pretend to own
    when really, universally,
we're all things each and never each alone.

The Wrong Tormented Sea

I am as dumb as anyone, of course.
    I just can't accept it. *Educate!*
they cried back in the 60s, with all the force
    of Magellan sailing through his strait,

he who discovered in the Phillipines
    one head is worth one coconut.
I've never learned to dwell within my means.
    Across my ship's top deck I strut,

assuming immortality will follow
    since I've surveyed the seas of Homer
and stomached all the Plato I could swallow,
    bellying up amid the foam or,

when tossed in rougher waters, Aristotle.
    I've stayed this course for years on end.
Yet aimless as a message in a bottle,
    barely afloat, I can't pretend

any longer I can see which horizon
    my navigators had in mind,
nor that the craft a person lives and dies in
    can outperform its paradigm.

Giving Up the Ghost

What ghost would I give up, were I
to give up, mostly, and release
my preternatural self—like dye
squeezed from ripened berries, or peace
from edicts meant to justify

perpetually warring armies? Maybe
I'd get hung up inside a vine,
or sucked in by some Parsi baby
or, poisoned from my own design,
ooze into fat, or spread as rabies.

That would be that.
                    But this, this would melt
away, no flesh left to be stashed
with keepsakes of the self I felt
should stay.
                    And as my body flashed
before me, as my corpse's welt

went long past healing, feeling gone,
heart hollow as a dyer's eye,
my soul a hole,
                    still I'd be drawn
to what I now know I rely,
with disembodied sadness, on.

Why I Am a Problem

I'm almost eight years older than my father
when he died, flying. He was thirty-six
and steered his plane into a fog bank. I'm,
despite my modesty, a man who'd rather
have more than one woman. It's not the sex
(although I think about that all the time)

but like an iris waiting for the bees,
my pistil's spry. Nor am I like some siren
who, having lured one fool, seduces others,
but as a good American I seize
whatever new material I can.
As much as I fault fathers I fault mothers

for granting their sons free range, while their daughters
are forced to grow hard shells, so not to lose
the corner of the sea they swim in. Men,
meanwhile, like porpoises in shallow waters,
insist on showing off, even as they bruise
from hitting bottom over and over again.

When women are themselves, will I be sorry
to waive the power of my size? Perhaps.
There's always something lost in gain.
My father, who wanted to go so far he
would never come back, flew dead into those traps
he'd been eluding. So like a weathervane

my body points away from pain behind me
more than toward the positive direction
I seem to blow in. No one must take blame,
though. Blame gathers like dust, until blindly
we brush it off, while what escapes detection—
love, say—drifts in the air, or goes down in flame.

Last Loss

"The music in my head," I said,
"I'll miss the most," counting my other losses
the way an undertaker counts the dead.
    Each obstacle I come across is

    about the same, about my pain,
while all those wonderful freak accidents
where love is fluid as a whooping crane
    swerve through my mind, their radiance

    immeasurable. Yet they, too, fade,
these melodies crowding my brain. Like sin
they are forgiven, even as they're made,
    are doors to rooms too dark to wander in.

Landscapes

Stump

A hollowed-out trunk in a field, a tree
I never knew—catalpa, maybe, or elm—
to us a shallow fort we soon outgrew,
it withstood a hard decade of winters.

Look at it now: fat stub, a small lump
stuck in my imagination, like a breadcrumb
brushed under table linen. Frost,
no doubt, had killed it, or who knows,

a rare pestilence of scarabs. Yet glued
still to the inside wall of my cranium
it remains somehow, faded, to be exhumed
like this, its jagged edges splintering

above that hide of snow we loved
to puncture with our boots, stumbling
into its core. And it has worn through
the years of my forgetting friends' names,

the total casualties of the Arab war: a
trace of nothing, a place where I scraped
my knee once, sat on its roots, and cried
(though who can recall what for).

The Day after Labor Day

Protected from the drifting August sun,
the woman with the child on the sand
smiled, then waved. Alone at twenty-one,
taking the breeze of autumn's breath that fanned
my sunburned shoulders, I paused to ignore,

then shrugged to show I saw, her. Then I saw her,
bending low to adjust her baby's strap
beneath their beach umbrella. I should've called her
to see her lift her body and unwrap
the towel from her thighs, to hear its *flap-*

flap in the ocean sounds surrounding us,
the shore abandoned, tide out, her husband gone
for the week, my parents having made no fuss,
as they drove off, about my staying on.
The sky wider than sex, the surf withdrawn

and shy, to see her running through her hair
her brown fingers, watch her baby clap and reach
to grab the breasts of her red bathing suit—I swear
if I could bring her back now, bring that beach
into this room, I'd make up for my breach

of faith that afternoon, and wouldn't lie
like this, hands clutched between my knees, blanched, June
past memory, the blue days of July
as distant as the promise of the moon,
September's seagulls calling, *not so soon so soon!*

Poem for Barbara

If not this year but several pass and you,
a blue and uneventful ocean view
lacking even the gesture of a sail
my mind might gather in in small detail,
still feel invisible, despite that I
intently gaze at you, as at the sky,
a breathless sky above the water, clear
and gentle in its rise, yet flush with fear,
don't think me self-absorbed, intransigent,
or cool. Were it enough to be content
with living with one whom I could recognize
as sometimes beautiful, or one whose eyes
assuaged my long-tormented soul, I'd say
as much—I'm tempted even now to stray
from my not saying such, to wax sublime,
to batten down your beauty with a rhyme
or two and let that be my celebration
not of you nor the sea, this brief vacation
from the truth, but of me for thinking so.
I can't dismiss what I'm not thinking, though:
You're not what I expected, so the shore
I stand on, as fragile as the weather, more
or less replaceable, depending what
the sea delivers, sinks into the rut
of its own undoing, *down, down, down.*
Whatever words set sail upturn and drown
under the waves of your otherness, while here
in the dormant air, I stare at what is near,
missing each arc, the muffled cry of gulls,
the shifting tides in you, the rage, the lulls.

My Mistake

We huddled from the rain under the sandstone abutment
outside the Lyndon Baines Johnson Library in Austin, Texas,
and I thought for a minute we were riding a train
along the coast near Rapallo, Italy,
with the summer sun slumping behind
the clouds and you in a thin
black-and-white striped travel dress
like Stefania Sandrelli's in Bertolucci's *The Conformist*,
as you described for me how you lost
your virginity, while I was of course so
understanding, and there was this other man
it seems I knew then who never
thinks of me now, I'm sure, and certainly at that moment
we all could have been in the movies, after
the desperate moisture of our love-making,
draining us, as it does, away from ourselves.
I should have married you that night.

Leaf Like Love

You have to clip this leaf that strains,
        this odd one twisting free
toward the light, whose arching veins
        draw moisture from the tree

        damaging its center.
The garden doesn't need its shade.
        Like love, it must be laid
aside, before, come late September

when nights grow cooler, stronger limbs
        you hope to keep alive
through winter you'll then have to trim
        to save. It will contrive,

        of course, to dazzle or dissuade you,
turn red with lust or rage. Ignore it.
        Like love, you can't restore it
and before you know it, it will fade.

After a Late Conversation in Winter

Her sad silent face seems tired now,
not like the time in June the sun subsided
behind her house and the pines soon

in shadowed groves began to congregate
along the border of her garden,
veiling the corners of her smile.

In that dusk we would have gone next
into her room, but in this haze we linger.
The street lamp lights up her tears

the same as, spilling suddenly under
clusters of boughs, the sun's rays did once
before, when I clung to her saying my name.

Two Mississippis

for Rebecca & Darryl

I

If the river is a woman who awakens
and splashes morning in her eyes, who stretches
her arms and dips them in the dance of dawn,
then combs her hair with sunlight, as she turns
and twists to listen to the brush of trees
beside her in the early breeze, who hums
and dresses delicately, easing her limbs
into her dappled skirt, her mottled sleeves,
who sips her tea then glides out to the gate
to greet the traffic passing there, and who
on entering the street begins to stray
a little, just a little (unaware
the obstacles her independent means
impose on those who'd rather she remain
inside and watch her flowers grow, not slow
their swollen progress to some venal shore),
then bends and wanders, when the weather's right,
and reaches toward the south, and, reaching, dreams
the dreams inspiring others drifting by
to catch her sparkle, taste her sigh, or slip
behind her gaze to swim inside,
                                    then who
are we? Her lover stealing from her bed,
deserting her with lies? Her child who,
ignoring how he's sucked her dry, sucks harder?
Her god?

II

And if the river is a man
rugged and brown, but round and muscular,
who wanders through the wilderness at dusk,
who plucks a fallen branch, then ambles on
between the trees, bowing and rising, who
at coming to a clearing scales a rock,
pausing briefly, rubbing his sides, then hums
and winds around the hills to wander down
into the pine grove on their farther side,
who feeds the beetles, beavers, birds, and bears
thinking him kind, who veers through twilit shadows,
their brilliance like a memory that flashes
and is gone, who tells himself those stories
that echo in the breeze they're carried on,
whose grey eyes pool when he beholds the sun
at last, and at the last who spreads his arms
to seize its light, then turns to go alone
once more in darkness, leaving in his wake
no sign of wandering there,

then who are we,
waiting in silence near his path, who strike,
then leave him on the forest floor for dead?
Are we, earth's thieves, so starved that we must bleed
the bled? Can no kind words for us be said?

After the Facts

What we think we have accomplished is real,
whereas what we in fact achieve melts away
like plastic under a window in the sun. It's no fun
pretending anymore, our thoughts buttoned like shirts
without grommets, that our lives are going places
and fast, steeped on this incline of wet ice.
Slick ambition can't steel us against the past.
I'm sorry.
              But the hard edge of suspicion breaks
over and over over my head, like a door made of glass
every time I turn around to look at what was there
or at the door itself, which I can see through
but walk directly into, and whatever I can't avoid
changes me, irrefrangible though I be. It's the same,
fortunately, for you and the rest. Just try and resist
and you will never be the same for having
finally come through, like that tower that withstood
the blast at Hiroshima. Desire will sow its own end
but to build around it another monument, transparent,
large, mutable and smooth, is to render
what is not ours, not letting what is ours be.

Munich Evening: After the Reunification of Germany

A culture based on joy is bound to be shallow.
—Derek Walcott

Will not our cult be founded on the waves?
Young couples stroll the Marienplatz, while the blues
surround these crumbling icons, draped in nets,
of well-dressed saints who saved this Church. Its nave's
empty now, except for homeless men and labor crews
mingling at dusk their curses and silhouettes.

By day this square sprouts business suits; by night,
lost ghouls, while the rest of us pass by and wonder—
pass by, pass by like *Völkerschaften* once who flocked
to see the Pope, the Kaiser or the haloed light
around the *Führer's* head. But wait. Hear that thunder?
The crowd's dispersing—all but those two, locked

into each other in the rain: He's black
as earth, her hair as yellow-brown as grass
craving water. Look close! They're getting drenched!
Her breasts soak through her blouse! He strokes her back
with hands as shiny as Venetian glass.
Owning no special grace, soon they too will be wrenched

apart, in search of shelter. But for now
let them float. Let all of us rise and fall
in numbers, or alone, crossing the shore
to our undoing. For now we need not bow
to God or nature, or the poor, nor crawl
to beer and wurst, nor talk in metaphor.

For now this sudden cloudburst of desire,
swelling the downspouts, cascades from the verge
I'm crouching under, as I wait for the end. . .
of what? Of floods? Of holocaustal fire?

Joy and despair, conspiring here, submerge
this shallow world I love, but can't defend.

July 1992

The Wandering of Amelia Earhart as a Model for Our Time

Knowing less than those who have gone before
provides us, co-pilots of the supposed, the power
at this stage in our history of guessing at,
as she did, the enigmatic bank of our next misty
turn, where it will deliver us after a slow descent
adrift over a waving cadre of amazed villagers
running like buffalo across a plain down there
through the haze. Their frenzy is as alluring
as those dark, quiet hills along that sun-fed horizon
or those bushy trees that cushion them, their branches
as abstract as veiled women, but even the summer night
falling onto us with the cold precision of a clock
in a cockpit cannot stop it, our benign future,
from drawing us further onward with its glow
of happy confusion. Like a fading star,
we will fly into that distant clearing
unknown, until we drop and roll through the fog,
never having to repeat ourselves, yet not to be
forgotten, in that unfamiliar way we've come to love.

Still Lives

spiriti questi? personae?
    tangibility by no means atasal
    but the crystal can be weighed in the hand
                         —Ezra Pound

Night Glimpse

An image fluttered just
now, beyond the corner
of my eye: A butter-

fly? A torn frond
of palm tossing in
the wind? A bright coin

no luck is spent with?
Slightly bent, then
gone, a cosmic ray

maybe, or like a thought
when I am drifting
at the end of day

and loss like light
vaguely interferes with
my private darkness,

it marks the limit
of rest, a breath of
what's out there, not

nothing, surely, but
consummate as air
or infinite beauty,

a small death early I'd
best not care for.

At God's Apartment

I knocked.

"There's no one home."

"But I can hear you."

"You can't. Your ears have fallen off."

"But near you
I smell your sweat."

"Not mine but yours. Besides,
your nose hairs are as thick as bamboo hides—
and before you tell me what you see, think blind."

"The door?" I asked.

"The problem with your kind
starts in your head, then spreads, soon to depart
southward to your crotch, bypassing your heart
and gut."

"I'm fed and don't require more."

"Then why in hell come knocking at my door?"

"A few ideas I've wanted to run by you
before my death."

"You have more time than I do
for small ideas and blessings."

"All the same,"

I said, persisting, "you have such a name
for pity."

       "I have lost my taste for those
like you, who'd always have me in the throes
of passion for the meek. I'm like the dead;
I lack your sweet embodiment."

             That said,
I touched the doorknob and began to turn,
hoping to catch a glimpse from which to learn
the nature of the warmth there.

           "You're too late,"
I heard inside.

      "Then how long must I wait
for you to come again to crack this door?"

"I guess your brains have fallen through the floor."

"But why," I cried, "why do I hurt this way?"

"Invisibility, that old cliché,
has folded you into its portmanteau,
so I'm afraid it's time for you to go."

"Where to? I can't fly off. I have no wings
nor any license."

      "What you're feeling stings,
I know. Embrace your old obscurity
and like the other millions you'll be free
from images of you you may not care for."

"But what exactly, then, should I prepare for?"

"Not to be taken in by what you're told."

I left the building, went out in the cold,
felt for my ears to put my earflaps on,
but I found nothing there. My ears were gone.

Conceit for My Cancer

The bottom of this well has dried up. Cup
the drops of water clinging to its side
in cool reserves of moss, before they slide
slowly down to the hollow spring, now muck,
that fed it once, and listen for the echo
of currents rising, falling away, hushed
in raw dank cadences where runnels gushed
before. Inhale the half-lush smell. Then let go,

please, of the caking residue of salt,
the damp clay cracking at its base, your breath's
pale face disintegrating in the blackness.
The bottom of this well may swell with brackish
sludge and wrack, rotting from death's cold sweats,
but please forgive me. This is not my fault.

No Elegy for One Who Died Too Soon

for Andrew Burkhard (1975–1992)

Some things escape us: useful days, free hours,
earned dollars, hats we shouldn't have stopped holding,
heat we hope will break in afternoon showers,
a shower inconveniently unfolding

itself like curtains let down from a rafter
on a giant stage that frames the street we pass
en route from work to home, from now to after,
the in-betweens, the images in glass

that two or three of us made once while strolling
downtown in that small city, out-flung ropes,
the smiles in photographs, the awkward calling
hundreds of miles across high wires, hopes

that snap, hopes that don't, stealing a nap
or listing in a boat—these get away
from us. But we're to blame for what has hap-
pened here. And we're to blame each time we say,

"Things get away," without then understanding
the ones who understand but don't know how,
the ones who sleep late, who have trouble landing
a job that pays, who wear their hats too low

pretending confidence, who brave a storm
to feel its penetrating blow, who sail
alone to kill the pain that keeps them warm.
Things get away. He won't come back.

Lines for an Obstinate Poet

for Raeburn Miller (1934–1990)

The aftermath of all your troubling looks
and grimaces (half posed as though from books
you once held dear, half unself-conscious), now
as those whose friendship you would not allow
are straining to remember, gives us hints
and guesses only—words, like fingerprints
which place you squarely at the scene, in rhymes
we puzzle over to reconstruct your crimes:

You robbed us of your passion when you died,
embezzled each one's patience you belied,
and left for those whose dignity you lifted
the empty touch of grace. How you were gifted
that way, cracking vulnerable hearts and making
off like a thief with their private treasures, taking
no hostages. You used words like tools
to ply the innocent and screw the fools,

and somehow, before now, you escaped the law
of being average, distorting every flaw—
your dread of being seen in public places,
the way you masked your eyes to shun the faces
of those you feared—into the hero's sin
of overzealous pride in discipline.
Safely hid out in the equitous cave of verse
you danced dark tarantellas to your curse,

until death, time's secret agent, pieced together
the clues of your grand larceny, and whether
by hook or crook, it traced you to your den,
then struck you down, then struck you down again,
granting no stay for you to testify
in self-defense. Death took you, stubborn, shy.

Only your poems survive. Only there you yield
those riches you so carefully concealed.

My Refusal to Despair

for Peter D' Agostino (1953–1988)

This small knot drawn
tight I can't untangle
from my throat I've
never found the
center of. When I first
passed the test—to
stand on my own—
you said, *Take care
not to slouch too
much*, so I prepared
to straggle along
alone, like an indoor
hanging plant. Since
then I find, at least,
that when I rant
I'm alive, not numb.

How will I know
to give in? When
reach the rust edge
of hope? Sound
as a solid country
house, I endure from
winter to winter,
only to slope in the
strident, mildewing
summer sun. Peter,
dear friend a dozen
years dead now and
more, teach me to loosen
and splinter. Tell me
how to be dumb.

Old Ghosts the Best

confuse the thing I see
—*Ezra Pound*

Why do I keep remembering my old ghosts
the best? That shade, for instance, like a flame
hovering by the boardwalk bench I sat on
the first night I considered suicide:
For me, at fourteen, nothing tasted sweeter.
Or posing in his bleak, black, rain-soaked cloak,

thin Pound at Brunnenburg, throat full of bold toasts
for every hamadryad he could name,
out by the terrace, with his broad-brimmed hat on,
leaning into his stick.
                              Who else? Poor Peter
before he died astonished, who went for broke,
stroking strange men at will on the Lower East Side?

I'm reeling from his visits still.
                                            Another day
in Princeton, gamboling on the playing fields,
I suddenly observed a flash of vision
like those I'd read about in Blake: Bright lights
began streaking across the lawn in gray,
indiscernible designs: Precision

suggests an image here, but my mind yields
nothing concrete, just small electric bites,
as though transparent bees had stung my eyes.
And no female ghosts yet, the tangible kind:
Instinct consigns them to my sleep, too real
to conjure.
                    But what of my father,
as faint as when I knew him? No surprise
the moment I've forgotten him I find
next to my bed a blot I neither feel

nor can describe, a blur I'd hardly bother
about, except it slips inside me, as I lie
placid and hard as sun-absorbing stone

yet pliant as the ice-age siege that formed me.
He never seems disturbed, though, lurking there
like some great overcoat, arms bearing sky:
whatever he confers freezes my bones
until I wake, when somehow it has always warmed me,
the way his trace replenishes the air.

When You Visit

Small angels, faint from ages
of counting others' blessings, come
when you visit. They rise

and opening their wings like pages
unshake their limbs from numb
death, taking light in from your eyes.

Paraclete Almost

J.M.W. Turner's Europa and the Bull

His own center cannot hold, so the god Zeus
becomes a beast, a bull. And as the beach
gives way under his hooves, it's by pure will
alone he lingers on the sand until,
submitting to that same chance offered each
of us, he finds himself among those bodies

familiar yet mysterious. Like me,
for instance, whenever I'm watching women
who walk along the water's edge to gaze
into the distance, past the blue black waves,
longing to loose themselves, and while I'm swimming
far from the shore, swept almost out to sea,

I recognize—as they bend toward their shells,
their knees wet with salt spray, their hair let down
untied, the breezy flexing of their thighs
transforming my indifference to surprise—
how easily I'm undone, how quickly bound
by sheer desire, and, as the darkened swells

swallow my slick gray bulk like a whale's,
how readily I would betray her I,
in that same moment, love more than the earth,
giving my every thought to. What's it worth,
languishing in this cove we occupy,
if we can't contract the empty space that pales

beside us, unconsoled yet always there?
The god, we're told, can no more shun our world
than we his, made bold by what weakens him.
So he lures Europa—lured, too, by those dim,
unsettled riptides past the breakers, curled
around his neck—to plead to the heavens, fair

and beautifully bright, to lift them both
above the ordinary ballast bodies,
afloat, depend on—to where they'll disappear.
Yet staring at this painting, lying here
all day, cannot explain my own odd, pleasing
attraction to this unfamiliar myth

I've come across too late. Neither god nor beast,
I hail from a long line of scattered bones,
determined sea lovers, and occupants
of temporary homes. I've not a chance
of finding myself one day in these dunes
next to Europa's friends, facing the east,

absorbed in yellows Turner never finished.
That figure in the foreground I can't see,
is she dancing? Arms raised in merriment,
or fear, she's virtually irrelevant,
a shadow, maybe, leaning toward the sea;
maybe he meant her even more diminished

than she appears, not to be contemplated.
Has he painted her out, not like a ghost
mindlessly enchanted by Zeus's charm,
but opposite to that, more to disarm
than dazzle us, a paraclete almost,
a wisp of an idea, dissipated

in the aftermath of what has happened there,
now left behind, her limbs stretched out in prayer,
something only gods can see, if gods can see
without succumbing to the same ache she,
like us, has suffered to become like air,
invisible and free? I wonder why I care.

For the Duration

The meaning of life is the wife
I can't leave. She has gone to school
so much longer than I have
the ambiance of our conversation,
after the evening chores have
absorbed the cool flood of food
we prepare like prayers for each other,
follows the smooth curve of her mind
more than mine. In most cases,
I feel fine about this imbalance.
Given over to her kind hands, I
fall into a trance I still recall
from the days when I would trace
the lines in her face, then play with
her breasts, while she would caress
my hair or my chest. We loved,
then, the power of clement time
newlyweds bring to their beds
like incense. We loved the scent
of rhyme like a tropical flower
blooming in just the right place.
But lately, she tires of my drift
toward the incidental, when
at home after dusk I spend hours
as though I were already dead, lifting
cold stakes of blame to drive them
into her staunch fidelity. Lately,
she finds my brain's paunch too fat
with baseless questions, their folds
impossible to exercise away. I try,
but she just tosses her intelligent curls,
dropping her head, and mutters phrases
I'll never understand. We're hopeless
together; we're perfectly matched.

About the Poet

Born in 1953, John Gery grew up in Lititz, Pennsylvania, and studied at Princeton, the University of Chicago, and Stanford. His previous books of poetry include *Charlemagne: A Song of Gestures* (Plumbers Ink, 1983), *The Burning of New Orleans* (Amelie, 1988), *Three Poems* (Le Stat, 1989), *The Enemies of Leisure* (Story Line, 1995), winner of a Critic's Choice Award and a "Best Book of 1995" citation from *Publishers Weekly*, and *Davenport's Version* (Portals, 2003), a narrative poem of Civil War New Orleans. His *American Ghost: Selected Poems* (Raska Skola, 1999; Cross Cultural, 1999), translated by Biljana D. Obradovic, an English-Serbian collection published in Belgrade, received the European Award of the Circle Franz Kafka in Prague. He has also published a critical book, *Nuclear Annihilation and Contemporary American Poetry: Ways of Nothingness* (Florida, 1996) and, with Vahe Baladouni, *For the House of Torkom* (Cross Cultural, 1999), an English translation of prose poems by the Armenian poet Hmayyag Shems. His awards include an NEA Creative Writing Fellowship, a Louisiana Artist Fellowship, and two Deep South Writers Poetry Prizes. A Research Professor of English at the University of New Orleans, he has also taught at Stanford, San Jose State, and the University of Iowa, and he is Founding Director of the Ezra Pound Center for Literature at Brunnenburg Castle, Italy.